John Dalton

John Dalton
the Founder of the Modern Atomic Theory

Prof. R. M. Wenley
A. B. Grifiths

LM Publishers

John Dalton was an English scientist known for his famous work in the development of modern atomic theory; and his research on color-blindness (daltonism), in which the affected person is unable to distinguish between red and green.

John Dalton and his achievement: a glimpse across a century[1]

It is a melancholy reflection that the treasure laid up by great men in our memories should be corrupted often by the moth and rust of error. But, after all, this mischance roots in the nature of the case. Necessarily, our views of the past are synoptic, because the daily details, even of big events, escape us, much more the complex, ceaseless pulsations of the persons who have served their time and place rarely. Be we appreciative or critical, we lie under sore temptation to forget the inevitable limitations of human lot, and thus to lose

---

[1] By Prof. R. M. Wenley

perspective. Accordingly, my scientific colleagues, with whom you have done me the honor to associate me in our effort to pay worthy homage to the genius of John Dalton (1766-1844), whose "A New System of Chemical Philosophy," although not completed in the second part of 1810, had reached all its epoch-making significance, have requested me to introduce the subject with some account of the difficulties, amazing to us in our conditions, under which this strenuous pioneer labored. To this end, we must try to pierce the cultural inwardness of English life at the close of the eighteenth century, keeping in mind the peculiar qualities that characterize English science even yet.

I

As usual, the bare facts of Dalton's story need interpretation, the invisible atmosphere, their setting, imports much. Born 1766, in a little village of Cumberland, a county still remarkable for its sparse population, of a Quaker family, who eked out a precarious livelihood upon the home industry of woolen-weaving, Dalton's social relations isolated him from the chief cultural organs of the national life.

Till the tender age of twelve he received such instruction as the local Friends' school afforded, and he appears to have made excellent use of his opportunities: then he went to work as a teacher there, and as a hand in the paternal fields, for three years. At fifteen he migrated — literally walked! — to Kendal, forty-five miles away, where he taught in a mixed school, the venture of a cousin; and, remember, a mixed, local school in the England of that generation portends not a little respecting absence of amenity, appliances and opportunity. Here he spent twelve years, fruitful in many respects. For, the day's darg done, he contrived to improve himself by private study of Latin, Greek, French, mathematics, and " natural philosophy/' with most important help and encouragement from John Gough 4 (1757-1825), the blind naturalist, celebrated by Wordsworth in "The Excursion."

> Methinks I see him how his eyeballs roll'd
> Beneath his ample brow, in darkness pained
> But each instinct with spirit, and the frame
> Of the whole countenance alive with
> thought, Fancy, and understanding; whilst
> the voice Discoursed of natural or moral
> truth, With eloquence and such authentic

power, That in his presence humbler knowledge stood Abashed, and tender pity overawed.

In 1793 he removed to Manchester where, on Gough's recommendation, he had been appointed science tutor in New College, a Presbyterian institution, and, therefore, once more without the pale of national higher education ; he held this position for six years, at a salary of $400. On the transference of the college to York, he resigned, and gave him- self to private tuition, an exiguous vocation, sufficient for daily bread. But the Manchester experience proved a turning point, for it offered an environment wherein he could make pure science his avocation. From 1786 Dalton had been engaged in meteorological observations, and published his maiden work in the autumn of 1793 — "Meteorological Observations and Essays." Printed for the author, it failed of due publicity.

Thanks to his connection with the Manchester Literary and Philosophical Society, he read his famous paper, "Extraordinary Facts Relating to the Vision of Colours," in October, 1794, a month after his election. In 1801 he presented his first classical research, " On the Constitution of Mixed Gases," which was followed by three memorable papers, " On the Force of Steam or Vapor from Water and other Liquids in Different Temperatures, both in a Toricellian Vacuum and in Air," "On Evaporation " and " On the Expansion of Gases by Heat." In the last he enunciated the law of expansion of gases formulated by Gay-Lussac a few months later.

It was in 1802, after six years of research in chemistry, that he referred to the possibility of multiple proportionate combinations of the elements, in a paper entitled "On the Proportion of the Several Gases or Elastic Fluids Constituting the Atmosphere."

The atomic symbols devised by him are first found in his note-book under the date September 6, 1803; and, under the same date there is a table of atomic weights, showing that, by this time, he had grappled with the fundamental problem — that of fixed " relative weights of the ultimate particles of bodies."

For unknown reasons Dalton appended it, in a some-what different form, to a paper "On the Absorption of Gases by Water," read before the Manchester Society in

October, 1803, but not published till November, 1805. The table was added during the interval between presentation and publication.

The summer of 1804, as Dalton himself tells us, was the crucial period of the investigation. The first part of the first volume of the "New System of Chemical Philosophy," published in 1808, gives the mature theory, while the second part of 1810 describes the chemical elements in detail. Dalton was now forty- four. And it is significant that, although he had lectured twice at the London Royal Institution, and in Glasgow and Edinburgh as well, the French Academy of Science recognized his merits six years 5 before any native body. In 1822, Dalton being fifty-six, the Royal Society honored itself by his election. Another decade elapsed ere Oxford conferred her D.C.L., on the occasion of the second meeting of the British Association, and he was sixty-eight when Edinburgh enrolled him among her honorary doctors. In 1833, the government took note of his services, and he received a civil list pension, increased afterwards in 1836, when the announcement was publicly made under dramatic circumstances by Sedgwick, at the Cambridge meeting of the British Association. " The imagination may picture, if it can," writes Roscoe, " the feelings of the son of the poor Eaglesfield handloom weaver as he sat in the Senate House of the University of Cambridge listening to this eulogium — the observed of all observers." 6 As Sedgwick remarked in his striking speech, " without any powerful apparatus for making philosophical experiments — with an apparatus, indeed, many of them might think almost contemptible — and with very limited external means for employing his great natural powers, he had gone straight forward in his distinguished course, and obtained for himself, in those branches of knowledge which he had cultivated, a name not perhaps equaled by that of any other living philosopher of the world." Evidently, then, Dalton wrought under grave disadvantages. What were they?

We would all agree, I take it, that certain results of human activity must remain intimately personal, and that, as a consequence, they must vary from age to age, or diverge even among different peoples in the same epoch. Art and poetry, religion and, possibly, some portions of philosophy, cannot well escape these very subtle contrasts. But, with Wissenschaft, particularly in that development of it known to us as positive science, the case stands far otherwise. Yet, even here, the unification of knowledge, each nation contributing its quota to the common fund, happens to be perhaps the achievement of the nineteenth century. Organization by countries, especially in the case of France, there was between the Renascence and the French Revolution; but a worldwide pact, embracing all effort, no matter where, did not eventuate then. Now, it is of prime moment for the present subject that the instruments of this recent unification have been the German university sys- tem, and the academies and institutes of France. By contrast, the English-speaking world possessed no such developed organs, if we except the Scottish universities where, naturally enough, Dalton met immediate recognition. Thus English science till but yesterday — teste even Darwin — has betrayed individualistic tendencies. These were never more evident than in Dalton's career, and during his life, moreover.

At the beginning of the nineteenth century, when Cuvier, in his "Rapport" of 1808, is extolling — and justly — the preeminence of France in the exact sciences, an extraordinary contract manifests itself across the Channel. In the same year, John Playfair bewails the "incontrovertible proofs of the inferiority of the English mathematicians," and refers to "the public institutions of England" as its cause. 8 Eight years later, in a damnatory notice of Dealtry's "Principles of Flux- ions," another writer notes it for a paradox that, Newton dead, his country "should, for the last seventy or eighty years, have been inferior to so many of its neighbours."

Once more, in the same review for 1822, a third critic deplores the state of affairs at Cambridge, where "for want of facilities" men "are apt to lose the spirit of investigation." Brewster's article in the Quarterly Review which, as is well known, led to the foundation of the British Association, is no less sarcastic and outspoken. These attacks were directed against the English universities: that of Babbage, the peg on which Brewster hung his exordium, had the Royal Society for its mark. Now the extraordinary thing is that, prior to and during these years, or, to be quite exact, between 1774 and 1828, Britain had contributed at least a dozen discoveries of the first magnitude, and as many more of scarcely less importance. As you all know for what each stands, I need only mention Priestley, Black, Landen, Davy, Benjamin Thompson, Cavendish, Herschel, Nicholson and Carlisle, Dalton, Young, Wollaston, Ivory, Bobert Brown, Charles Bell, Brewster, William Smith, Prout, Faraday, George Green and Bowan Hamilton. Still more wonderful, continental leaders were well aware of these contributions, and wont to emphasize them. In 1821, Cuvier gave most generous testimony: and Moll, of Utrecht, repelled Babbage's criticisms with no uncertain sound, remarking, "all must allow that it is an extraordinary circumstance for English character to be attacked by natives and defended by foreigners."

Although I cannot comment upon the ramifications to-night, the puzzle has some obvious causes. The English universities were not scientific organs, but groups of residential colleges. The advancement of science was no primary part of their purpose, precisely as the laborious elevation of incompetents to a bare level of possible passability was no primary part of the purpose of the German universities or the French institutes. The colleges cherished their individuality fondly, because they aimed to produce a certain type of man for life — to anneal him by forming his ethos, and to fit him for the exercise of civic influence by giving him a respectable general acquaintance with the "things of the mind." In a word, the English universities did not exist to promote science or learning, any more than the continental organizations existed to provide an educational top-dressing for the sons and daughters of "the people." So, too, of pure thought. The apostolic succession of English philosophers — Bacon, Hobbes, Locke, Berkeley, Hume, the Mills, Spencer, even our contemporaries, Hodgson, Balfour, Shand, Haldane and Bertrand Russell — do not adorn the universities. Again, the peculiar position of the metropolis, its new university in the melting-pot at this moment, must be taken into account. Lacking the academic center, its scientific societies could not be organized for the advancement of discovery after the style of French and German associations.

These causes, together with the distinctive arrangement of English society a century ago, tended to render the great scientific pioneers lonely figures, sitting loose to the main expressions and modes of national culture. The wails over the condition of English science are traceable as much to this severance, with its absence of constant intercourse and cooperation, as to aught else. How Priestley and Dalton and Joule, Young and Davy and Faraday were hampered by these circumstances is notorious. Others, like George Green, received no recognition whatsoever. In addition, the English passion for independence played its part. The demand for complete freedom, if it fostered the eccentricity of which the docile, drilled Germans complained, although it led to pig-headedness, as in Dalton's case, also proved greatly favorable to original genius. For, it is well to recall that more original notions, basal to modern science, have come from England than from any other land, even if, as with Newton and Darwin, France was to systematize Newtonianisme, Germany Darwinismus.

England possessed no trained regiments to accomplish these things. Accordingly, if we remember all this, some apparent mysteries that cloak Dalton's career and mental characteristics begin to dissipate. In short, the Dalton we commemorate would have been nigh inconceivable had he been "born to the intellectual purple of the ancient universities " ; but the Dalton we regret, who remained obdurate to Gay-Lussac despite Berzelius's intercession, might never have been. The qualities of the man, like his defects, pertained to his strong, wayward and un- disciplined, if narrow and often uncouth, provincialism. *Qui a nuce nucleum esse vult, frangat nucem.*

II

Dalton maintained silence from 1793 till 1799, hindered, perhaps, by college duties. On reappearance, he soon dropped the role of meteorologist for that of chemist and physicist. The new line was taken in the paper entitled "Experiments and Observations on the Power of Fluids to Conduct Heat, with Reference to Count Rumford's Seventh Essay on the same Subject," read before the Manchester Society on April 12, 1799. The simple nature of his apparatus may be illustrated aptly from this communication.

Took an ale glass of a conical figure, 2i inches in diameter, and 3 inches deep; filled it with water that had been standing in the room, and consequently of the temperature of the air nearly. Put the bulb of a thermometer in the bottom of the glass, the scale being out of the water; then having marked the temperature, I put the red-hot tip of a poker half an inch deep in the water, holding it there steadily for half a minute; and as soon as it was withdrawn, I dipped the bulb of a sensitive thermometer about J inch, when it rose in a few seconds to 180°.

Then follow the tabulated temperature results. Another experiment, described in the same paper, suffices to show that Dalton had pondered the discontinuity of matter thus early. Having mixed hot and cold water for half a minute, he proceeded to determine whether the upper layer became warmer than the lower. Observing that it did not, he remarked : " If the particles of water during the agitation had not actually communicated their heat, the hot ones ought to have risen to the top, and the cold ones subsided, so as to have made a material difference in the temperature."

Furthermore, these and many other experiments afford us indications of his mental habit as a scientific investigator. Conceptual processes find him at his best; his theoretical expectations and deductions are good. In experiment he is not so happy, and what we understand by "fine" or refined work occurs seldom. Thus, in the case just cited, Dalton infers "that the expansion of water is the same both above and below the point of maximum density." But, when he comes to determine this crucial point precisely, he goes wide of the mark, setting it at 36°.

These references may enable us to grasp his manner of approach to a problem, and to realize his general plan of attack upon the atomic constitution of matter as it stood when he entered the field.

I wish that space permitted me to present some consecutive account of the doctrine of "matter" as it developed down the ages — but this is impossible. The subject deserves attention, because so bemused in the minds of the laity. And not only this. Scientific men themselves misconceive it at times, not deliberately indeed, but because, absorbed in researches of immediate moment, they have not troubled to follow the marvelous story with patience. The long, tortuous endeavors that culminated in Dalton's atomic theory, with its kernel, the law of multiple ratios, are the tale of man's attempt to reduce his notion of "matter" to conceptual simplicity ; this to the end that it might be rendered an obedient instrument. Freed from contingent accessories, the central problem was this: Given such a vast multiplicity and variety of phenomena as the "substantial" world presents, how can all be grasped under a single, synthetic idea? Plainly, whenever man began to reflect upon nature, he encountered this sphinx. The elusive, yet persistent, relationship between the one and the many forms part of ancient history in science no less than in metaphysics.

Now, stating the situation very synoptically, and omitting the meta-physical reference in favor of the natural-scientific, it may be affirmed that the problem itself is also a many in a one. For, if we are to reach clear concepts about natural phenomena, we must reckon with three investigations at least. In the first place, a particular phenomenon must be selected, and treated as the starting point.

This done, it is requisite to obtain an all-round view of what it is. In the second place, one must proceed to elucidate its relations to other phenomena, preferably to those which evince evident, or apparent, kinship. In the third place, order must be induced in the relations that have thus come under observation by reducing them, as far as possible, to numerical expression. The primary methods of weighing, measuring and enumeration must be invoked. This achieved, we may assert that we have arrived at that species of conceptual simplicity which we call a "law of nature." On a broad view, it is fair to say that, prior to Dalton, investigation and fancy pursued the one (i. e., the conception of "matter") through the many (i. e., these three aspects of the problem). For, on the whole, till we come to J. J. Becher (1635-82) and G. E.

Stahl (1660-1734), the element theory held the field. And this is only to affirm that men were trying to master the properties of particular bodies, while reserving the remoter question of the ultimate constitution of "matter." Roger Bacon's view, probably the least fantastic we possess, is exceedingly significant of this.

There are four Elements— fire, water, air, earth; that is, the properties of their condition are four— heat, coldness, dryness and wetness; and hyle is the thing in which there is nor heat, nor coldness, nor dryness, nor wetness, and a body is not. And the Elements are made of hyle; and each of the elements is transmuted into the nature of the other element and everything into everything else. For barley is a horse by virtual possibility, that is, occult nature; and wheat is a man by virtual possibility, and a man is wheat by virtual possibility.

The age of phlogiston, with its theories of combustion, marks a move to the second question. Men are now engaged in an effort to relate phenomena. Or, as Stahl puts it, in his conspectus : Combustible substance minus phlogiston is burnt substance — e. g., metals, sulphur, phosphorus, etc., minus phlogiston, are metal calxes, sulphuric and phosphoric acids, etc. On the other hand, burnt substance plus phlogiston is combustible substance — e. g., metal calxes, sulphuric and phosphoric acids, plus phlogiston supplied by carbon, are metals, sulphur, phosphorus, etc. In a word, the most different phenomena, such as the burning of carbon and the calcination of a metal, are shown to belong to the same class, and to be explicable by a simple conceptual hypothesis. Finally, when Lavoisier sent phlogiston by the board, the third question came to the fore, and men began to ask, How can we weigh, measure and enumerate the exact degree of relationship between the properties of substances? Dalton ranks among the great epoch-makers, because he first brought this inquiry within the range of practicable uniformity.

Discussions about prior discovery, over which much time and no little temper have been expended, prove profitless affairs, as a rule. You see, error and loyalty are human. For instance, I am well aware that scientific chemistry is dated usually from 1776, when Lavoisier made the balance the chemical instrument: but you will bear with Sadler and me if we travel a little farther back and, as loyal sons of alma mater, find the initial point in the classical investigation of latent heat, conducted by Black between 1759 and

1763, at Glasgow. Nevertheless, as Dalton's priority has been impugned, we are bound to consider the facts.

Of course, everyone knows that the conception of the discontinuity of "matter" appears in ancient history. And, when we descend to modern times, Boyle (1627-91) speaks of corpuscles, Boerhaave (1668-1738), Albrecht von Haller's master, of massulce. Moreover, Dalton was a youth of only seventeen when the most important developments occurred. First, and with special reference to the framework of possible method, we have Lavoisier's (1743-94) celebrated memoir, "Reflections concerning Phlogiston," where he dismisses the dominant theory in sarcastic terms, and establishes the quantitative method on a firm basis. In the same year (1783) Bergman (1735-84), the last of the great phlogistic chemists, published his notable work on what he called "elective attraction" (i. e., affinity), a phenomenon attributed by him to the attraction between the most minute particles. Naturally, Bergman's table of "single elective attractions in the moist way, and in the dry way," with its curious alchemical signs, was a description of qualitative relations. It marked the beginning of investigation of mass action, and provoked the striking researches of Berthollet (1748-1822), who, in 1799, presented his paper, "*Recherches sur les lois de l'affinit*é," out of which grew his major work, "*Essai de statique chimique* " (1803). The main result of his assault upon Bergman was to show that chemical change depends, not merely upon the affinities of the substances involved, but upon their quantities. In other words, a new method asserted itself. For, as Berthollet says :

> To find the affinity of two substances towards a third, in accordance with the conception we have now gained of affinity, can mean nothing other than to determine the ratio in which this third substance divides itself between the two first.

Therefore, chemical change hinges upon the nature of the relative masses of the substances involved, but, "to determine the ratio of the affinities of two substances towards a third ... is attended by unsurmountable obstacles." Here was the blank wall, so to speak, that shadowed Berthollet's services till the time of Guldberg and Waage (1864). As Berthollet stood to Bergman, so did Proust (1755-1826) to Berthollet. Baffled in every attempt to determine the distribution of salts in solution, Berthollet had good reason to doubt the doctrine of constant composition. Here was Proust's opportunity. Having distinguished between "combinations of elements" and "associations of combinations," the latter variable under analysis, Proust was able to enunciate the law of fixed proportions — in his own words, "Election and proportion [i.e., affinity and fixity of composition] are the two poles about which revolves immutably the whole system of true com- pounds, whether produced by Nature or by Man " ; or, as Lothar Meyer phrases it, "Definite chemical compounds always contain their constituents in fixed and invariable proportions."

Notice, in the words I have italicized, the unanimous trend towards quantitative measurements and accuracy, the ruling notion being that of numerical ratio. We come to closer quarters with our central theme in the work of Richter (1762-1807), an investigator, it is important to note, obsessed by mathematical methods. Despite his obvious idiosyncrasy, Richter arrived at the law of equivalent ratios — "The qualities of acids and bases equivalent in one neutralization are equivalent in all." In 1802 Fischer made Richter's conclusions known to Berthollet, and chemical ratios became an integral part of the science. As Wollaston says, in 1814:

> It is to Richter we are originally indebted for the possibility of representing the proportions in which the different substances unite with each other in such terms that the same substance shall always be represented by the same number. He discovered the law of permanent proportions.

The experimental proof was clinched by Berzelius in 1811-12, and the law of "permanent " or "definite " ratios, as it is called now, put the problem of composition on a practicable footing.

It should be noted also that, in stating the numerical values of the elements, Dalton employed some determinations of other chemists, at all events as checks.

We are now in a position to see that series of complicated researches, all looking to quantitative results, furnished Dalton with material which enabled him to render the atomic theory perspicuous and applicable from the very outset. Notwithstanding, to him must be given sole credit for the final simplification, which had been exercising his mind for some eighteen years — since 1790, in fact. A quotation from Berthollet's "Essai" (1803) may suffice to emphasize the long step due to Dalton's insight.

> Some chemists, influenced by having found determinate proportions in several combinations, have frequently considered it as a general law that combinations should be formed in invariable proportions; so that, according to them, when a neutral salt acquires an excess of acid or alkali, the homogeneous substance resulting from it is a solution of the neutral salt in a portion of the free acid or alkali. This is a hypothesis which has no foundation, but a distinction between solution and combination.

Undoubtedly, events tended towards the new climate of opinion, nay, this had become so far prevalent that the Irishman, William Higgins (17?-1825) came nigh playing Wallace to Dalton's Darwin. Indeed, in 1814, he raised a claim to priority, which was disproved at once by Thomson, the Glasgow chemist who had made Dalton known. This Higgins is to be distinguished from his uncle, Bryan Higgins (1737-1820), who, in 1775, in a prospectus of lectures, proposed to discourse of "his notions and experiments concerning the primary elements and properties of matter," and of "experiments, observations and arguments, persuading that each primary element consists of atoms homogeneal: that these atoms are impenetrable, immutable in figure, inconvertible, and that, in the ordinary course of nature, they are not annihilated, nor newly created."

He also conceived of atoms, of simple particles, and even of gases, as uniting sometimes, in approximately, if not completely, fixed proportions. Yet, he never arrived at true causes, because his experiments failed to dovetail with his advanced theoretical suggestions. Accordingly, the explicit variety of the former destroyed the implicit unity of the latter, and the status quo ante was maintained.

William Higgins, the claimant of 1814, published his book 22 in 1789. It contains forecasts of the atomic theory, such as the following :

> I am likewise of opinion that every primary particle of phlogisticated air is united to two of dephlogisticated air, and that these molecules are surrounded with one common atmosphere of fire.

But, after all, less than a dozen pages of the 300 deal with the subject; and, although he assigned causes for definite proportion and saturation in a few cases, he never suspected a simple, universal and necessary law. His real acuteness led him to see that combining particles had the same weight (multiple proportions), but he missed his chance to generalize in a maze of suspicions directed against the phlogistic theory, which had already lost its primacy; his indolence also hindered him, like his eccentricity.

III

Finally, coming to Dalton's characteristics as a thinker, we may find the clue in his forcible independence. In the preface to Part II of "A New System of Chemical Philosophy" (1810), he declares:

Having been in my progress so often misled, by taking for granted the results of others, I have determined to write as little as possible but what I can attest by my own experience. On this account, the following work will be found to contain more original facts and experiments, than any other of its size, on the elementary principles of chemistry.

Here the strong man places himself on record, and the question of priority takes to flight. Accordingly, I state it as my clear impression that the merits and defects of his achievement are alike traceable to the fact that our laureate lay under direct obligation to but one of his predecessors — Newton. Dalton encountered certain phenomena, such as multiple and definite proportion, aqueous vapor as a distinct constituent of air, and, seeking for the simplest common representation, found it in Newton's well-known doctrine. For example, he says :

According to this view of the subject [heat], every atom has an atmosphere of heat around it, in the same manner as the earth or any other planet has its atmosphere of air surrounding it, which cannot certainly be said to be held by chemical affinity, but by a species of attraction of a very different kind.

And he quotes from Newton :

All bodies seem to be composed of hard particles. . . . Even the rays of light seem to be hard bodies, and how such very hard particles which are only laid together and touch only in a few points, can stick together, and that so firmly as they do, without the assistance of something which causes them to be attracted or pressed towards one another, is very difficult to conceive.

This was the secret of the opposition of Hope and, later, of Faraday's complaint. In a letter, dated January 2, 1811, Hope wrote to Dalton as follows :

I need not conceal from you that I am by no means a convert to your doc- trine, and do not approve of putting the result of speculative reasoning as experiment.

While Faraday, similarly suspicious, as late as 1844, said:

The word atom, which can never be used without involving much that is purely hypothetical, is often intended to be used to express a simple fact. . . . There can be no doubt that the words definite proportions, equivalents, primes, etc., . did not express the hypothesis as well as the fact.

The truth is that Dalton was a first-rate theorist, who arrived at his conclusions, not primarily on the basis of induction from experiment, but by reflection. Analogically, he imports the view of "matter" peculiar to celestial mechanics, through molecular physics, into the realm of chemistry. Proceeding thus deductively, he evinces little awareness of the very complex problems involved, which the later developments of the atomic theory were to reveal. Cut off from the world, he did not possess intimate acquaintance in detail with the labors of his immediate predecessors and contemporaries — a happy accident, no doubt. For, this freedom from puzzle and disturbance enabled him to proceed boldly with a generalization when men of the caliber of Wollaston and Davy hung back. Dalton had natural capacity for logical thought, and complete confidence in the validity of those mathematical syntheses of physical facts which he had pondered.

But, as happens frequently, his limitations are traceable to the same source. Like Kant before him, Dalton became so entangled in the theoretical ways of his own thought that, after he had promulgated his theory, he stopped short in middle life, and could not appreciate the work of others who followed and supported him. This is the blot on his' scutcheon. Still, even so, we must hold the balance true. The kinetic doctrine of "matter," integral to the Cartesian philosophy, had paled before Newtonian atomism. And Dalton had grasped Newton's view so logically that he could not admit the law of equal volumes, because, as he held, "no two elastic bodies agree in the size of their particles." The very success of his hypothesis blinded him to Gay-Lussac's experimental evidence — it would not conform to the conceptual scheme. As he wrote to Berzelius, in September, 1812 :

> The French doctrine of equal measures of gases combining, etc., is what I do not admit, understanding it in a mathematical sense. At the same time I acknowledge there is something wonderful in the frequency of the approximation.

Of course, the fact was that, as Wurz points out,

The relation which exists between the densities of gases and their atomic weights is not so simple as we should at first sight be led to expect, and as for a long time it was thought to be.

Nay, "understanding it in a mathematical sense," Dalton had his reasons. By a kind of paradox, the very simplicity of his notion befogged him here, just as the problems bred of the atomic theory diverted chemists for many a long day from the study of affinity.

We may conclude, then, that the logical character of Dalton's mind enabled him to formulate the timely conceptual representation on which chemical logic has pivoted ever since; that his numerical conception has stood the test of further discovery better than most hypotheses; and that, little as he knew it, or could admit it at the moment, he laid the foundation for that intimate alliance between physics and chemistry which forms one of the most pregnant among contemporary movements. For, the active criticism of the atomic theory — that it dogmatizes about the physical constants marking the differences between the elements, that it reveals little or nothing of the processes incident to chemical composition and destruction, that it neglects synthesis — testifies also, if negatively, to the revolution wrought by its author. Pity is akin to praise here. And to-night, as we celebrate Dalton's " thoughts that breathe," we are bound to let praise have its free way, especially when we contemplate the indomitable devotion of a character who, amid sore difficulties, but furnished with the splendid spur of consecration to the ideal, achieved so much for man's conquest of the secrets of nature.

Short Biography of John Dalton[2]

John Dalton, the son of Joseph and Deborah Dalton; and he attended the village schools until he was eleven years of age. He was a steady-going, thoughtful, and industrious boy.

In 1778 he began to teach in a school at Eaglesfield, but had great trouble to maintain discipline owing to some of his pupils being as old as himself.

Disputes were often settled by exhibitions of physical force displayed in the neighbouring churchyard. Three years later he gave up the school, and went as assistant to his cousin, George Bewley, at

[2] Based on the article of Arthur Bower Griffiths published in *Biographies of Scientific Men*.

Kendal, which position he occupied four years. At the end of this time Bewley retired, and the school was continued by the brothers, John and Joseph Dalton, but as teachers they were not popular owing to their uncouth manners.

After leaving Kendal, Dalton went to Manchester as a science tutor to the Manchester New College then existing in the city, and afterwards as a private tutor of science and mathematics. "As a schoolmaster he began life, as a schoolmaster he ended it," but such routine work was not the sole occupation of his mind—far from it.

His scientific *Observations upon the Weather* were begun on 24th March 1787, and continued until the day before his death (*i.e.* for over half a century).

JOHN DALTON AND HIS TOMB
IN MANCHESTER

JOHN DALTON AND HIS TOMB IN MANCHESTER

In 1794 Dalton was elected a member of the Literary and Philosophical Society of Manchester, and for fifty years he spent his time, in a room of the Society's house in George Street, in teaching, writing, and studying.

His first paper, in 1794, was *"Extraordinary Facts relating to the Vision of Colours."* Dalton had a defective colour sense, which was amusingly confirmed by thc prcsentation to his mother of a pair of scarlet silk stockings when he was under the impression that they were drab. On another occasion, when selecting cloth for a new suit of clothes, he requested a drab material; a piece caught his eye, and he remarked that it was just what he required, but the tailor informed him it was scarlet cloth for hunting coats.

About this time he published a book on *Meteorological Observations and Essays*, recording the connection between the aurora borealis and electricity, on the dew-point, thermometers, barometers, etc.

In 1799 he proved that aqueous vapour exists in the atmosphere. In 1800 he published a paper on the conducting power of water for heat; and in 1801 appeared his *Constitution of Mixed Gases*, wherein he proved "the total pressure of a mixture of two gases on the walls of the containing vessel is equal to the sum of the pressures of each gas; in other words, that if one gas is removed the pressure now exerted by the remaining gas is exactly the same as was exerted by that gas in the original mixture."

It may be mentioned that among Dalton's pupils was the celebrated James Prescott

Joule (of the "mechanical equivalent of heat" and the "conservation of energy" fame). Both tutor and pupil are in the first rank of scientific investigators, and hence Manchester has the perhaps unique distinction of having been the home of two of the greatest natural philosophers who ever lived.

John Dalton, the Quaker philosopher, was the founder of the atomic theory, and this great generalization is one of the foundation-stones of modern chemistry.

Leucippus appears to have been the first to grasp the idea that matter is composed of ultimate particles or atoms. Democritus of Abdera (born 460 B.C.) developed the atomic theory of Leucippus, and stated that atoms were impenetrable and indivisible. Epicurus (born 340 B.C.) gave mobility to the atoms, and otherwise greatly improved the atomic theory of the Greek philosophers. According to these sages "the world is composed of an innumerable quantity of atoms, mobile, infinitely small, and distant from each other." These ideas were nothing more than a brilliant speculation.

The atomic theory remained a speculation for over two thousand years, until Dalton discovered the law of mutiple proportions, and deduced therefrom that matter is composed of atoms having weights, and that the atoms are of various kinds. When atoms of the same kind come into juxtaposition, elements are formed, such as oxygen, hydrogen, chlorine, etc. Compounds are formed from the juxtaposition of different kinds of atoms, such as water, ammonia, carbon dioxide, etc.

This is not all: to Dalton's law of multiple proportions, the law of Avogadro is adjoined. The latter law establishes that all gases, temperature and pressure being equal, have the same elastic force. As this force is probably due to the shock of atoms or groups of atoms (molecules) on the sides of vessels which contain the gases, it is evident that equal volumes of all elementary gases contain the same number of molecules or atoms. And, finally, Dulong and Petit proved that the *atoms* of the elements all possess the same specific heat. All these laws, which were the result of observation and experiment in the early part of the nineteenth century, have converted into a scientific theory the ideas of the philosophers of ancient Greece.

Dalton's laboratory was in the lower rooms of the Manchester Literary and

Philosophical Society, and "was never remarkable for neatness. ... His bottles were of every shape, size, and colour, and his apparatus was of the most humble and inexpensive description. He often performed experiments at the cost of a few shillings on which others would spend as many pounds." What wonderful results were obtained with such meagre appliances! It may be asked whether the laboratories of Lavoisier, Priestley, and Dalton, with their meagre appliances, produced better work than the luxuriously-fitted laboratories of to-day. The question is not easily answered. It must, however, have been simply delightful to have worked under Lavoisier, Priestley, or Dalton, each a genius and pioneer in the early days of modern chemistry. Lavoisier and Dalton were the architects of a new chemistry—a chemistry which has stood the test of time, and is of the greatest value to all nations—in fact, the "wealth of nations."

In 1803 Dalton published a paper "*On the Absorption of Gases by Water and other Liquids.*" This memoir had an important bearing on Henry's law discovered in the same year.

The first account of Dalton's famous atomic theory appeared in Thomson's *Chemistry* in 1807, he having told Thomson of his experiments and deductions. In 1808 Dalton published his *New System of Chemical Philosophy*, in which the theory of atoms was fully expounded; and he described experiments directed towards the estimation of the relative weights of atoms. The numbers he obtained as representing the atomic weights were in many cases erroneous; but they were rectified by the work of Berzelius (1779-1848), and even now these constants of nature are subject to frequent revision. It was, however, to the genius of Dalton that the atomic weights of the elements were first comprehended.

Since Dalton's time, the sizes, intervals, and velocities of atoms have been ascertained. These problems have been solved by Clausius, Kelvin, Clerk Maxwell, and others from various sides: "from a comparison with the wave-lengths of light, with the tenuity of the thinnest films of soap-bubbles just before they burst, and from the kinetic theory of gases, involving the dimensions, paths, and velocities of elastic bodies, constantly colliding, and by their impacts producing the resulting pressure on the confining surface." For instance, one cubic centimeter of air contains twenty-one trillions of molecules;

the average distance between each molecule equals ninety-five millionths of a millimeter; the average velocity of each molecule is four hundred and forty-seven meters per second; and the average number of impacts received by each molecule is four thousand seven hundred millions per second.

In 1865 Loschmidt of Vienna, twenty-one years after Dalton's death, calculated that the diameter of an atom of oxygen was the one-ten-millionth of a centimeter; and Kelvin came to the conclusion that the distance between the centers of contiguous molecules is less than the one-five-millionth and greater than one-thousand-millionth of a centimeter.

All this work has been the outcome of Dalton's atomic theory. Sir George Darwin says that "within the last few years the electrical researches of Lenard, Röntgen, Becquerel, the Curies, Larmor, Thomson, and a host of others have shown that the atom is not indivisible (as Dalton assumed), and a flood of light has been thrown thereby on the ultimate constitution of matter. Among all these fertile investigators it seems that J. J. Thomson stands pre-eminent, because it is practically through him that we are to-day in a better position for picturing the structure of an atom than was ever the case before. It has been shown that the atom really consists of large numbers of component parts. By various converging lines of experiment it has been proved that the simplest of all atoms, namely, hydrogen consists of about three hundred separate parts; while the number of parts in the atom of the denser metals must be counted by tens of thousands. These separate parts of the atom have been called corpuscles or electrons, and may be described as particles of negative electricity."

As Professor Rutherford says: "It is not true that the discoveries of the last ten years had weakened the atomic theory. On the contrary, they had enormously strengthened it." It is an error to suppose that recent research has removed Dalton's atomic theory or rendered it obsolete. We now know that Dalton's atoms are not atoms, but it is still true that "elements combine in constant proportions by weight." In the words of Sir George Darwin: "The vast edifice of modern chemistry has been built with atomic bricks." From the later work of to-day we know that the atom is not the ultimate form of matter. There are corpuscles and ions inconceivably smaller; but, says Professor A. Smithells, "few will deny that the atomic theory stands to-day an indispensable instrument for productive work; it has neither had its day nor ceased to be. We are now called upon to subdivide our atom, to credit it with an unsuspected store of energy, to consider it a congeries of unsubstantial electrons. There can be no possible objection from our side; it will undo nothing that has been done, and we may have good hopes that it will lead to the doing of many new things in chemistry."

In 1802 Dalton ascertained the composition of the atmosphere, namely, that a hundred volumes contain twenty-one volumes of oxygen and seventy-nine volumes of nitrogen. In 1804 he was asked to give a course of lectures at the Royal Institution of London; and in these lectures he explained his views on the absorption of gases by liquids, on the constitution of gases, etc. As a lecturer, his manner lacked charm and gracefulness, but in spite of these defects his genius was greatly appreciated.

He was a man of great industry, perseverance, and modesty. "It was with difficulty that he accepted any of the numerous honours proffered him. At first declining to become a candidate for the F.R.S., he was elected in 1822 without his knowledge." In 1830 he was elected one of the eight foreign associates of the *Académie des Sciences*, and in 1832 Oxford University conferred upon him the degree of D.C.L.

In 1822, Dalton visited Paris. Here he met many distinguished men, among whom may be mentioned, Cuvier, Laplace, Gay-Lussac, Arago, Biot, and others.

In 1836 William IV., on the recommendation of Lord Melbourne, granted Dalton a civil list pension of £300 a year.

In 1834 he received the degree of LL.D. from Edinburgh University.

Dalton's private life was monotonous, and to a certain extent uneventful. His character "was most amiable, simple, and unostentatious." His life was in his work. Science was everything to him. The chief recreation in which he indulged was bowls; he belonged to a bowling club which met at the Dog and Partridge Tavern in Manchester. Dalton was of medium height, robust and muscular; his voice was gruff, and his manner curt. When asked why he never married, he replied that he never had time (most likely impecuniosity was the primary cause). He was not, however, totally indifferent to the influence of women, for a warm friendship existed between him and Miss Nancy Wilson. The lady died young, but he always cherished her memory with affection. Another valued friend of Dalton's was Mademoiselle Clementine Cuvier, the daughter of the celebrated naturalist.

Concerning Dalton's atomic theory, it may be stated that he introduced the idea of weights—his theory is essentially one of weight—the relative weights of the different atoms. The first public notice of the atomic theory is contained in his paper, "*An Experimental Inquiry into the Proportion of the Several Gases contained in the Atmosphere*." He found that oxygen has the power of combining in two different proportions with nitric oxide, forming two distinct bodies, and that the quantities by weight of oxygen which combine are in the simple ratio of one to two. No intermediate compound could be obtained. It was this fact that led to the atomic theory, and the law of multiple proportions. "It is to Dalton—who made his living by giving private lessons at half a crown each—that we owe this knowledge which has made the fortunes of thousands, because he first told us the laws which govern chemical action."

Dalton's atomic theory is, however, somewhat different from the one of today. In his day the smallest particle (elementary or compound) was an atom, whereas now compound bodies are composed of atoms of the elements which form the compounds, and are termed molecules. The molecule of a compound contains *different* atoms, whereas the molecule of an element contains the *same* atoms.

Although not an accurate manipulator (who could be with such crude apparatus at his disposal?), he was a philosopher, a deep thinker, yea, a genius. He was gifted with that most useful "article"—scientific imagination. "He formed clear mental images of the phenomena which he studied, and these images he was able to combine and modify so that there resulted a new image containing in itself all the essential parts of each separate picture which he had previously formed."

In 1837 his health began to fail and his mental powers to decline; he had a paralytic seizure, but afterwards recovered to a certain extent.

When fainting Nature called for aid, □

And hovering Death prepared the blow.

Johnson.

Seven years later he had another attack, which proved fatal on 27th July 1844. With public honours his remains were buried in Ardwick Cemetery, Manchester; and a massive tomb of red granite marks the spot where the founder of the atomic theory lies buried.

Of posthumous honours, there is a beautiful statue of Dalton by Sir Francis L. Chantrey in the vestibule of the Manchester Town Hall; and in the same building there is a fresco, by Madox Brown, representing Dalton collecting methane or marsh gas from a stagnant pool. Opposite to Dalton's statue is one of Joule, by Gilbert. These two statues are the most beautiful sculptures Manchester possesses, and they commemorate the life-work of two men who are to the northern city what Shakespeare is to Stratford-on-Avon, or Kelvin to Glasgow. In addition to these honours to Dalton's memory, there are the Dalton chemical and mathematical scholarships awarded by the authorities of the Owens College, Manchester; and a street in Manchester bears his name.

*

To conclude, the "atomic theory," in the words of the celebrated French chemist Wurtz, "has thrown light upon the most recent discoveries, as it has been, since the time of Dalton, its immortal author, the most perfect instrument in the most profound theoretical conceptions, and the safest guide in experimental researches."

.

18647711R00045

Printed in Great Britain
by Amazon